POCKET CAMERA
HANDBOOK

Series editor
Michael Langford

EBURY PRESS

The Pocket Camera Handbook was conceived, designed
and edited by **Dorling Kindersley Limited,** 9 Henrietta Street,
London WC2

Technical adviser **Adrian Holloway**
Writer/researcher **Lucy Lidell**

Project editor **Joanna Godfrey Wood**
Art editor **David McGrail**
Designer **Debra Lee**
Assistant designer **Calvin Evans**
Managing editor **Joss Pearson**
Managing art editor **Stuart Jackman**
Editorial director **Christopher Davis**

Titles in the *Basic Photography Series* may share some common illustrations
where visual techniques shown apply to all photography and are not
restricted to specific equipment.

First published in Great Britain in 1980 by Ebury Press,
National Magazine House, 72 Broadwick Street,
London WIV 2BP.

Second impression 1982
Copyright © 1980 by Dorling Kindersley Limited, London.

ISBN 0-85223-170-9

Printed in the Netherlands by Smeets Offset B.V., Weert

Contents

Introduction

This is a practical handbook for people with pocket cameras. Recognizing the needs of amateurs, it avoids technical language or costly special equipment. Instead, it concentrates on the heart of good picture-taking: how to get the best out of your camera, and avoid mistakes; how to take advantage of light, color, viewpoint, and timing; and how to develop a photographer's eye for effective subjects.

Pocket cameras are light, small, and easy and quick to use. With today's quality lenses, color films, and flash equipment, you can take pictures in a wide range of conditions, with excellent results. Most of the pictures in this book are attainable with any pocket camera — all of them with a good 35mm compact model.

But to get the best out of your camera, you have to know its potential and limitations. Most pocket cameras have largely automatic controls, and many have a limited exposure range. Nearly all have a non-removable lens. And most important of all,

the viewfinder, which shows you the scene, is quite separate from the lens, which actually takes the picture. So you cannot see in advance how the camera controls will affect your picture.

All these points are covered simply in the first part of this handbook, "Using your camera" (gray page borders). It looks at typical pocket cameras, helps you to choose films and flash, and

takes you through basic routines for handling your camera and taking pictures.

The second section, "Getting better pictures" (red borders), shows you how to use viewpoint, lighting and composition, and gives simple, practical advice on handling moving subjects, night shots, and flash pictures.

The third section, "Handling different subjects" (yellow borders), looks at common picture taking situations, from family groups and weddings to views and foreign vacations. Using tips, comparisons, and specially commissioned photos, it shows you how to make the most effective use of your camera, subject and location. The last section (gray borders) covers faults, accessories, advanced cameras, and picture presentation.

The Pocket Camera Handbook will help you to get more pleasure and use out of your camera, and better results every time. We hope it will set you on the road to an absorbing, round-the-year hobby.
Michael Langford

Camera Basics

A **camera** is a light-tight box with a hole in the front covered by a lens. The **aperture**, adjustable in size, makes the hole larger or smaller, controlling the amount of light entering the camera. The **shutter** controls the time the light is allowed to act on the film.

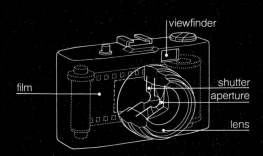

The product of the combination of aperture and shutter is called **exposure**. The **lens** makes rays of light from the subject converge to form an image on the **film** (held flat in the back of the camera). The **viewfinder** is a separate window which lets you compose your picture.

The 110 pocket camera

Weather symbols

Shutter release

Tele lens slide

Camera back release

Flipflash socket

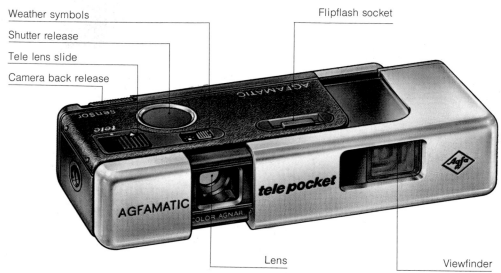

Lens

Viewfinder

The 110 is the true "pocket" camera. Typical models have the classic flat shape and are small, lightweight, quick to load and simple to use. Common features on medium priced models are shown below. More costly models may have a better lens, a focusing rangefinder and/or automatic exposure. Small negative size and a tendency to camera shake are the two main disadvantages of 110s. To minimize camera shake, many models have a "sensor" shutter release (see below) and some are now made in the traditional "upright" shape. Others have steadying handles.

Common 110 features

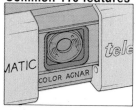

The lens
This is commonly recessed behind a square opening, which is flush with the camera. Some lenses are fixed-focus; others have a range of focus symbols (p. 19). Some have a slide-over tele lens to enlarge the scene (p. 85).

Weather symbols
Exposure is often set by symbols — sun, hazy sun, cloud and flash (p. 20).

Flash
Many models accept flash bars as well as their own electronic units (p. 22).

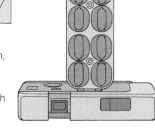

Viewfinder
The viewfinder generally has a brightline inner frame, close-up correction marks (p. 18) and often a low light warning (p. 21). If there is an extra lens, the view changes accordingly in the finder when it is in position.

Shutter release
An electronic "sensor" release requires little pressure to fire the shutter and so reduces the possibility of camera shake.

Film

110 cameras take film cartridges which have a larger spool at one end. The negative is small (11×17 mm), allowing limited enlargement — typically to about post-card size, as shown here. The quality of enlargements depends on the quality of the lens and the care you take in holding the camera still. Slides come back from the processor in small mounts. But you can obtain larger mounts, which adapt 110 slides for ordinary 35 mm projectors. The range of films is not large, as shown by the chart below.

110 films

ASA	Color print	Color slide	B/W
64		•	
80	•		
100	•		
125			•
400	•		

Loading the film

Loading 110 film is very simple — it is impossible to put the film in the wrong way round *and* close the camera back. The cartridge is light-tight before and after use, but, for safety, you should load and unload out of direct sunlight. Don't remove the cartridge once the film is in use. If you do, you may spoil (fog) several shots. Each cartridge has its own take-up spool to receive the exposed film. After the last frame, you don't have to rewind — you just remove the whole cartridge. For the best results try to get your film processed as soon as possible.

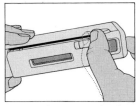

1 Open the camera back. Take care that the lighting is not bright.

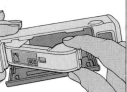

2 Put in the cartridge, inserting the larger spool first. The label on the cartridge must be the right way up.

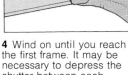

3 Make sure the cartridge is pushed in flat before you close the camera back.

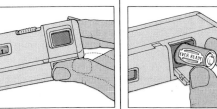

4 Wind on until you reach the first frame. It may be necessary to depress the shutter between each winding stroke.

Batteries

These power the metering or electronic flash system. They last about a year, but you must remove them if the camera is not used over a long period. There are two ways of testing the battery, if you have no test button.
1 With built-in flash, check the flash-ready light.
2 With an electric "eye", depress the shutter halfway and check if the viewfinder warning light comes on when you cover the "eye".

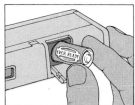

When loading a new battery, hold the camera upside down, with the door opening downward, as shown above.

The 35 mm compact camera

Hot shoe

Shutter release

Viewfinder

Film rewind

Frame counter

OLYMPUS TRIP 35

Light meter cell

Lens and controls

Flash cable socket

35 mm compact cameras fill the gap between the simpler and lighter 110 and 126 models and the heavier but more versatile SLRs. A typical 35 mm camera is still relatively light, but it offers much more control over picture quality. Its main advantage over both 110s and 126s is the wide range of films (see facing page) and accessories available. More expensive models may incorporate built-in flash or a choice of manual or automatic exposure, even sometimes autofocus. Advanced models compare favorably in quality with similarly priced SLRs.

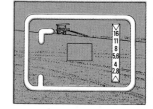

Typical 35 mm features

The lens
The lens on a 35 mm camera projects from the body. It carries the ASA setting dial (p. 15), plus focusing symbols and/or a distance scale (p. 19). Some lenses show shutter and aperture settings as well.

The metering system
Most 35 mm cameras have a built-in metering system which automatically adjusts the exposure. Exposure is measured by an electric "eye" or other light-sensitive device on the lens or camera body, as shown below.

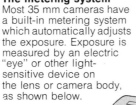

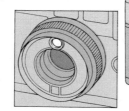

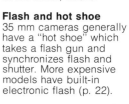

Viewfinder
A typical 35 mm viewfinder has a brightline frame with close-up correction marks (p. 18). It displays exposure settings, with warning lights to indicate under- or overexposure. Many cameras have a coupled rangefinder system (p. 19), shown in the central section of the finder, above.

Flash and hot shoe
35 mm cameras generally have a "hot shoe" which takes a flash gun and synchronizes flash and shutter. More expensive models have built-in electronic flash (p. 22).

Film

35 mm film has three main advantages over both the other formats — it is cheaper per shot; its image size (24×36 mm) allows bigger enlargements without loss of sharpness; and there is a wider range of 35 mm film types and speeds on the market. However, the film is packed in cassettes rather than easy-load cartridges.

35 mm films

ASA	Color print	Color slide	B/W
25		•	
32			•
50		•	
64		•	
80	•		
100	•	•	
125			•
160		•	
200		•	
400	•	•	•
1250			•

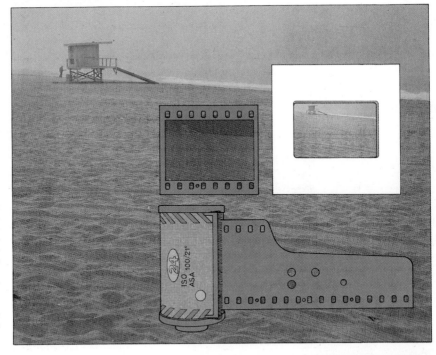

Loading and unloading

In general, 35 mm film is slower to load and unload than 110 or 126 film. Some cameras have an easy-load system. Most load according to the system shown in the step-by-step diagrams, right. Always load and unload your film in the shade. Never open the camera back once the film is in position and wound on in the camera — you may lose several exposures.

Batteries

Most 35 mm cameras with an automatic exposure system use small button-shaped batteries to power the light cells. Always keep the camera in its case to prevent battery power loss. Some cameras with built-in flash use the same batteries for both exposure and flash systems. Others require a larger battery to power their flash system. Test the battery regularly (p. 9).

1 Hold the camera firmly and open the back. The door should spring open. The latch is often positioned on the base, as shown.

2 Lift up the rewind knob and put the cassette in the left-hand chamber. Then push down the rewind knob so the cassette is held firmly in place.

3 Pull the film leader tongue out and insert it in the slot in the take-up spool. Wind the film on so that both rows of perforations are engaged on the sprockets.

4 Close the camera back and advance the film three frames or until "1" appears in the exposure counter window. Now set the ASA.

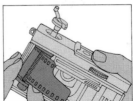

5 To unload, release the rewind button, fold out the crank in the rewind knob and turn it clockwise until it goes slack.

6 Open the camera back and take out the film. *Never open the camera back before you have rewound the film.*

The 126 simple camera

Flash cube socket

Shutter release

Viewfinder

Weather symbols

Flash distance

'INSTAMATIC' CAMERA

Kodak

REOMAR

Lens

The 126 camera shares the classic 35 mm shape, but takes cartridges not cassettes. The main virtue of this format lies in the large size of the film (see below). Most models are fixed-focus and many have only one exposure setting. More advanced 126s have a range of weather symbols. Most cameras take flash cubes only; a few also accept flash bars.

Film
The large image size (28×28 mm) gives sharper enlargements than 110 film. Like 110, 126 film comes in easy-loading cartridges. Unlike 110, a 126 cartridge is inserted with the larger spool on the right. 126 slides fit a standard 35 mm projector.

126 films

ASA	Color print	Color slide	B/W
64		•	
80	•		
100	•	•	
125			•
160		•	

Special features

If you are buying one of the more advanced new cameras, consider which of these special features would be most useful for your kind of photography. For instance, if you are likely to take a lot of action shots, choose a camera with features 3, 6 and 9. For night photography, look for a model with features 2 and 6. All the features below are built in to the camera. (Some may also be available as attachments.)

1 Alternative lenses
Format: 110 only
- Tele — candid portraiture and animals (p. 50, 84).
- Wide-angle — interiors and panoramic views (p. 55, 80).
- Zoom — gives choice of lens view and image size; unusual effects in action shots.
- Close-up/macro — allows you to shoot small subjects e.g. flowers, birds, as shown right, and possessions.

6 Built-in flash
Format: 110 and 35 mm
- Makes photography possible in any lighting conditions (p. 22).

7 Facility for off-camera flashgun
Format: 110 and 35mm
- Off-camera flash gives more flattering lighting for portraits (p. 33).

8 Flash set with focus
Format: Any with variable focus and aperture
- Allows you to vary flash exposure to suit a range of subject distances (p. 23).

9 Motor drive or autowind
Format: 110 and 35 mm
- Winds on automatically, allowing you to shoot continuously. It is useful for taking fast action sequences or capturing the fleeting expressions of candid photography (p. 50).

10 Self timer
Format: 110 and 35 mm
- Delays exposure for 10-15 seconds after shutter is depressed, enabling you to take a self portrait or to include yourself in a group picture (p.70).

2 Tripod socket, cable release time exposure
Format: 110 and 35 mm
- Tripod socket and cable release minimize camera shake (p. 17) at slow shutter speeds.
- Time exposure is useful for dim light and night shots, as shown right, when you want to keep the shutter open (p. 35).

3 Variable shutter speed
Format: mainly 35 mm
- Allows control over subject movement — you can either freeze moving subjects or blur them for emphasis (p. 36).

4 Variable aperture
Format: 110 and 35 mm
- Allows control over depth of field (p. 19), giving you the option of sharpness throughout your picture, or a sharp subject with an out-of-focus background, as shown above.

5 Exposure hold or override
Format: 35 mm only
- Enables you to take accurately exposed pictures (pp. 20–21) even with camera and subject in different lighting, or with back-lighting.

Choosing your film

There is a wide variety of films on the market, but deciding which one to use should not be a problem. The main things to consider are: do you want color prints, slides or black and white? Will you be shooting in dim or bright light? Do you prefer a particular color effect? For example, Ektachrome is bluer and Kodachrome is redder. It all depends what kind of shots you want to take. When you find a film you like, stick to it most of the time, changing only for a special reason.

The virtues of prints, slides or black and white are listed right. The aesthetic qualities of color and black and white are discussed on pp. 38-41.

Buying a film

When you go to buy a film it will help if you can interpret the coding on the pack.

Check the following points:
● Size — 110, 126 or 135 (35 mm)
● Type — color print, slide or black and white; suitable for daylight/flash or tungsten light (see facing page)

● Speed — ASA/DIN/ISO numbers (see "ASA setting", facing page)
● Number of exposures — 12,20,24 or 36
● Expiry date
● Whether the price includes processing

Film speed

A film is given an ASA number to show how sensitive it is to light. The higher the number, the more sensitive it is and the faster it reacts to light. Fast film therefore requires less light to take a picture. For most daylight shots use a medium speed film (64 to 125 ASA), but for dim light use a faster film (200 to 400 ASA for color, 400 ASA and over for black and white). For really poor lighting conditions, see p. 41. You can get very slow film for slides (25 to 50 ASA) and black and white (32 ASA).

Medium speed film is used for general photography in normal daylight or bright lighting conditions.

Fast film is used for dim light, interiors, dusk, fast action and distant flash photographs.

Slow film can be used in bright lighting. Its freedom from coarse grain allows enlargements full of detail.

ASA setting

Most 110 cameras, if they accept different speed films, adjust automatically for the film speed — the cartridges carry a coding notch which alters the range of exposure settings when you insert the film in the camera. You can see the ASA number on the cartridge, top right, through a window on the camera. You must adjust the film

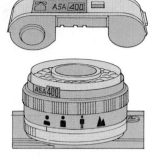

speed on all 35 mm (and some 110) cameras, by setting the ASA dial, bottom left. On a 35 mm camera the ASA number is marked on the film cassette, but you cannot see it once the camera back is closed. Try sticking the relevant part of the film pack on to the camera back to remind you of the ASA number. Check regularly that the ASA dial has not slipped.

If you notice that the ASA dial has slipped round to the wrong setting:
1 Shoot the rest of the film at the same setting.
2 Make a note of the wrong setting.
3 Enclose a note to your processor stating the incorrect ASA number and asking for your shots to be corrected. Check with your retailer for the name of a laboratory offering this service.

Which film?

Most people use color prints for convenience — you can look at them easily, display them in albums or frames and have them duplicated. But if you invest in a good projector and screen, slides offer brilliant color, greater realism and the pleasure of an evening slide show. Black and white films are cheaper, fun to experiment with and easy for home darkroom work. You may do best to use a mixture: color prints to record family events and to send copies to friends; black and white to experiment with new picture ideas; slides to illustrate a special holiday. Be sure you always use fresh film and have your pictures processed promptly.

	Prints	Slides	Black and white
Cost	● Most expensive	● Cheaper per shot	● Cheapest
Quality	● Realistic; fair color and sharpness	● Extremely realistic; brilliant color	● Less realistic; more abstract; fine detail, wide tonal range
Viewing and storing	● Easy in albums and frames	● Projector and storage system necessary as slides are easily damaged	● Easy in albums and frames
Duplicating and enlarging	● Easy; can be cropped, framed, etc	● More expensive to have prints made. Duplicates of slides lose quality	● Very cheap to duplicate and enlarge; easy for home darkroom work
Type of light	● Gives accurate color in most lighting except fluorescent	● Accurate color with daylight or flash: avoid room lights (or use "tungsten" film or a filter)	● Any light
Exposure errors	● Less likely to show errors as prints are given some correction	● Extra care must be taken with exposure	● Least likely to show errors as it is easiest to correct during printing
Speeds	● Only two generally available; medium (80 to 100 ASA), or very fast (400 ASA)	● Wide range of speeds available in 35 mm film, from 25 to 400 ASA	● Wide range of speeds available, up to ultrafast (1250 ASA) for low light

Color accuracy of films

Most color slide films are designed for use with daylight or flash. In artificial light you will get various color casts on slides unless you correct with filters or use special film.
● Filters affect exposure, so you must adjust it (p. 90). On metering cameras, make sure the filter covers the "eye" too.

■ Yellow/red cast Cause: domestic lamps. Use 82A, B or C filter, or try tungsten film.

■ Blue cast Cause: snow, dusk, deep shade under blue sky. Use 81A, B or C filter.

■ Green cast Cause: fluorescent lighting. Use Kodak's FL-W filter.

Holding your camera

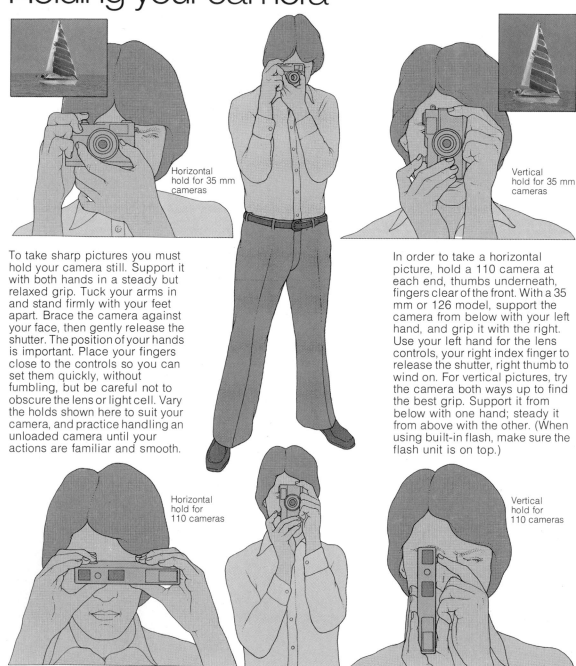

Horizontal
hold for 35 mm
cameras

Vertical
hold for 35 mm
cameras

To take sharp pictures you must hold your camera still. Support it with both hands in a steady but relaxed grip. Tuck your arms in and stand firmly with your feet apart. Brace the camera against your face, then gently release the shutter. The position of your hands is important. Place your fingers close to the controls so you can set them quickly, without fumbling, but be careful not to obscure the lens or light cell. Vary the holds shown here to suit your camera, and practice handling an unloaded camera until your actions are familiar and smooth.

In order to take a horizontal picture, hold a 110 camera at each end, thumbs underneath, fingers clear of the front. With a 35 mm or 126 model, support the camera from below with your left hand, and grip it with the right. Use your left hand for the lens controls, your right index finger to release the shutter, right thumb to wind on. For vertical pictures, try the camera both ways up to find the best grip. Support it from below with one hand; steady it from above with the other. (When using built-in flash, make sure the flash unit is on top.)

Horizontal
hold for
110 cameras

Vertical
hold for
110 cameras

Avoiding shake

The lighter your camera, the greater the danger of camera shake. This is the main cause of blurred or crooked shots, like those shown below. Take extra care with 110 cameras, as the small negative must be sharp for a good print.

Find a support

To minimize camera shake, look for a support for your body. Lean against something solid, or rest your elbows on a flat surface. For low viewpoints, sit with your elbows on your knees, or lie full length, supported on your elbows. *Check through the viewfinder that the camera is steady.*

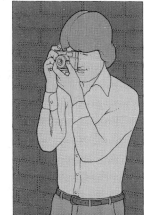

Lying support

Sitting support

Leaning support

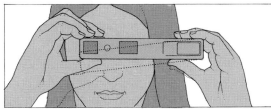

Tripod support

Press the shutter gently

You must release the shutter very gently if your pictures are going to be sharp. Keep your index finger just above, not beside, the shutter release button. Hold your breath, or breathe out steadily, and press the shutter release button with the cushion, not the tip, of your finger. If you jab the release, or press too hard, you may push one side of the camera down as you take the picture. The result will be tilted verticals and horizontals, and blurred shapes.
Move only your finger tip, not your whole hand.

Support the camera

In dim light, your shutter speed will be slow, and you must avoid touching the camera during exposure. Some cameras warn you of this with a light in the viewfinder. Below 1/60 sec, stand the camera on a table, or set it up on a tripod, and use a cable release.

Viewing and focusing

The viewfinder shows you the approximate picture area seen by the lens when you aim your camera. Your first film will show you how accurate its framing is. Many cameras have a brightline frame, far right, marking the exact field of view. But the image you receive through the finder may sometimes differ from the picture seen by the lens. The finder will give a sharp, bright image even if you have not set the controls. And because of the difference in view between the finder and the lens, you will not know if you have obscured the lens or, with close-up shots, cut off part of your subject, see below.

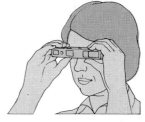

A typical viewfinder will show a sharp, well-framed picture, as above, even if you have neglected to focus or compensate for close-up framing, as left.

Correct eye position
Make sure that you can see all four sides of the viewfinder frame. If your eye is too close or too distant, your picture will contain less (or more) than you expected. If off-center, your subject will appear too near to one edge.

Eye to one side

Eye too close

Eye too far away

Framing close-ups
When you photograph subjects closer than about 6 ft (2 m) the difference in viewpoint between viewfinder and lens (shown right) may lead to "parallax error". To compensate for this frame your subject off-center in the direction of the lens, e.g. if your lens lies to the right of your viewfinder, frame your subject nearer the right edge. Some cameras provide parallax compensation marks, far right.

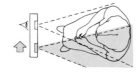

Horizontal error — finder beside lens. Mostly 110s.

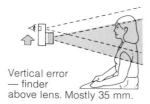

Vertical error — finder above lens. Mostly 35 mm.

Parallax error result

Corrected framing

▲ Use the "land-scape" symbol for main subjects 15 ft (5 m) or more away. With a distance scale, focus on midground. Only set ∞ if you want the foreground out of focus.

Use the "group" symbol for subjects 9-15 ft (3-5 m) away. With the camera held horizontally, most finders encompass a whole figure at 11 ft (3.5 m).

Use the "head-to-hips" symbol for subjects which are 6-9 ft (2-3 m) away. Watch out for intrusive background objects.

Use the "portrait" symbol for subjects 3-6 ft (1-2 m) away. Remember to compensate for parallax error and set focus accurately.

Take care not to go closer than the minimum focusing distance for your lens. NB Check the manual for your camera's exact setting.

The chart above shows the focusing symbols you should use for subjects at a given distance from your camera. The simplest cameras have "fixed focus" lenses that render everything acceptably sharp from about 6 ft (2 m) to infinity. Most cameras have adjustable lenses that need to be accurately focused to produce sharp pictures. Some have click-stop slides or rings with three or four symbols. Others have a focusing ring on the lens marked in feet and meters. If you find it hard to estimate distance, use the symbols and scale above as a guide.

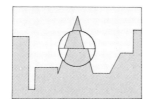

Rangefinders
Some cameras have a "rangefinder" coupled to the focus control, for fine focusing. When the lens is out of focus, the subject will appear either as a double image ("coincident" type) or in two halves (split image) in the center of the viewfinder. An unbroken image shows correct focus.

Depth of field
The zone of sharpness both in front of and behind your subject is called "depth of field". When you focus on a subject more than 10 ft (3 m) away, top right, most of your shot is sharp. With near subjects, right, the zone of sharpness is reduced; the back-ground may be out of focus. This can be useful if it is cluttered. Depth of field is also affected by aperture (p.21).

Getting the right exposure

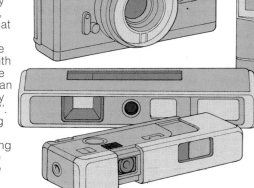

Nothing is so disappointing as pictures spoiled by wrong exposure — dim slides, muddy prints (underexposed) or weak, pale images (overexposed). What causes such errors? With a "point-and-press" camera there may have been too little light. With weather symbols you may have chosen the wrong setting. With an automatic, light conditions may have fooled the camera's "eye". Cut down mistakes by knowing your camera's exposure range and recognizing different lighting conditions. And check that the exposure is right for your *main subject*.

"Point-and-press"
Simple cameras have only one exposure setting. With medium speed film you can only safely shoot sunlit subjects. If in doubt, use flash. But with 400 ASA film you can shoot in shade, cloud or back-lighting.

Using weather symbols

This symbol is for bright, clear sun falling directly on a subject from the front.

This symbol is for hazy, misty sun, the weaker sun of late afternoon, or sidelit scenes.

This symbol is for cloudy, overcast scenes. You can also use it for subjects in shade, early evening or backlit scenes.

With 400 ASA film you can shoot on the cloud setting in dimmer light — indoors, dusk, dawn, or deep shade.

Which symbol?

Before setting the camera, look carefully at your main subject. Is it in the same lighting as the general scene? Is it in sun, shade or overcast light? Is it lit from the front, back or side? Look particularly at people's faces — these are usually the most important part of your shot.
Then choose the symbol that matches the main subject most closely.

This shot was taken on the sun setting, as it was a sunny day. But the *subject* was largely in shade, so is underexposed.

The same shot, taken on the cloud setting, is now correctly exposed. You can see much more detail, particularly in the face.

This subject was lit by the sun from behind. You must use the cloud symbol (or flash) if you want more detail than a silhouette.

Metering cameras

Metering cameras have an "eye" to read the light, and set exposure automatically. Some also allow override, or choice, of settings. All types display some exposure information in the viewfinder. You may have to depress the shutter lightly to activate the displays. If a warning light shows:
- Low light — use tripod or flash
- Underexposure — flash or a "time" exposure
- Overexposure — don't shoot (unless you are able to adjust your camera's aperture)

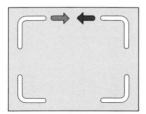

Backlit subjects

The "eye" tends to misread subjects lit from behind or placed against a bright sky. The subjects are facing away from the light, but the "eye" has direct light falling on it. The result is very underexposed and the figures are thrown almost into silhouette. To get detail in the subjects, shade the "eye" from above with your hand. Or (if your camera allows this) read the exposure close to the subject and keep it on that setting while you move farther back to take the photograph.

Read for the subject

These shots were taken with an automatic camera. The small one is underexposed — the photographer made the mistake of shooting in the sun when the subject was sitting in the shade under the picnic umbrella. The "eye" read the general sunlit scene, not the shaded subject. To take the larger shot the photographer moved into the shade himself, closer to the subject, so that the "eye" read correctly.
Always check that the "eye" is in the same lighting as the subject.

Aperture and shutter

Aperture (lens opening) and shutter speed control exposure. They also affect sharpness — wide apertures may blur backgrounds (they reduce depth of field, p. 19). Slow shutter speeds blur movement (p. 37). Aperture is scaled in "f stops" from f2.8 (wide) to f16 (small), shutter speed in seconds from 1/30 (slow) to 1/500 sec. A one-stop change on either scale halves (or doubles) exposure.

Wide aperture

Slow shutter speed

How flash works

Flash is essential with a pocket camera. Its "portable daylight" lets you shoot anywhere — indoors or out, by day or night, with the simplest of cameras. Recognizing this, manufacturers design the cameras for ready use of flash, often marketing matching flash equipment, or models with built-in flash. Check carefully which flash your camera takes. There are two main types: bulbs (in cubes or bars), and electronic (built-in or as separate "guns"). Some cameras use one flash type only — but often you can use either one type of bulb, or one of a range of guns. Electronic flash is worth the cost if used often.

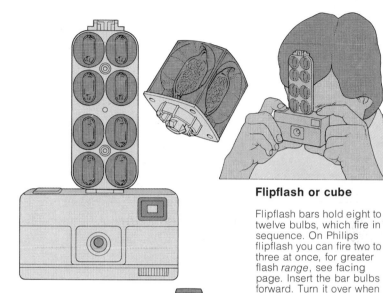

Flipflash or cube

Flipflash bars hold eight to twelve bulbs, which fire in sequence. On Philips flipflash you can fire two to three at once, for greater flash *range*, see facing page. Insert the bar bulbs forward. Turn it over when half the bulbs are used.

Cubes hold four blue bulbs. The cube rotates as you wind on, until a fresh bulb faces front.

Before you buy, check which makes of bar or cube your camera accepts.

Built-in flash

Both 110 and 35 mm models are now available with built-in electronic flash, powered by batteries. You get up to 200 flashes per fresh battery. When you set the flash switch, the flash pops up, and a "ready" light pulses when it is ready to fire. The unit normally takes about eight seconds to "warm up" between flashes. Check this before buying; long waits can be annoying. Recycling time increases as batteries run out — renew them regularly.

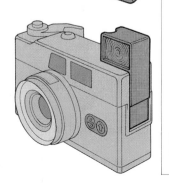

Flash units

On 35 mm models and some 110s the flash unit fits in a "hot shoe" on top. On others it fits in the side, with a lead to the "shoe". Recycling time is important (it must equal firing time on a motor drive). Units which you can use off camera give you much better lighting control.

Keep within flash range

Flash light loses strength with distance — to get good pictures you must stand close enough to the subject. With medium speed film, the effective flash range is usually from 3 to 9 ft (1 to 3 m) (check your model). Don't use flash closer than 3 ft (1 m), you may dazzle people and shots will be "bleached out". Increase flash range by using faster film or firing several bulbs at once. *Doubling film speed increases the range 50%, firing two bulbs at once increases it 40%.*

Range with 100 ASA film

3 ft (1 m)　　　　9 ft (3 m)　　　　18 ft (6 m)

Range with 400 ASA film

Avoid flash fall-off

The group above is all within flash range, but the rear figure looks too dark. Subjects twice as far from the flash receive only one-quarter as much light, right.

When taking group shots with flash, make sure all the members are roughly the same distance away — in the middle of the flash range, right. Then the lighting will appear even, above.

Setting the camera

On some models, switching to flash programs the camera to adjust aperture as you focus. This varies the effect of the flash to suit the subject distance. Switch to flash and then set the focus. If you have electronic flash, you must be sure to wait for the "flash ready" signal, above.

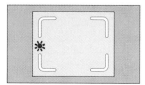

This shot was within flash range, but focus was set for farther away. The camera chose a wider aperture, causing overexposure.

The same portrait taken at the correct head-and-shoulder setting is now properly exposed. The camera selected a small aperture.

Flash exposure

Some sophisticated guns can vary flash power/duration. But with most flash this is fixed (indicated by "guide numbers"). To vary the flash effect you must change the camera aperture. Most pocket camera flash systems do this for you, as shown left. But on a few you select it yourself. Divide your subject distance by the guide number given for your film speed, to get the right aperture in f numbers. Many units carry a scale you can use to avoid this calculation.

Before you press the shutter

1
Set the controls

Before you take a picture check that you have set the controls on your particular camera. Have you:
- Set the ASA for your film?
- Set the correct focus symbol?
- Set the right weather symbol for the main subject?
- Checked for a low-light warning when you press the shutter halfway down?
- Switched to flash, if needed?

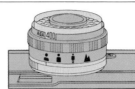

2
Check the camera front

The lens and the viewfinder are separate on a pocket camera. You will not be able to tell by looking through the viewfinder whether the lens or electric eye are obscured. Are you obscuring the lens or electric eye with:
- The lens cap or slide cover?
- Your finger or hair?
- The camera strap or case flap?

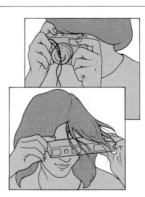

3
Look around the frame

Finally, look around the viewfinder frame and make sure that your picture will not be spoiled by one of these common errors:
- Is your eye position correct?
- Are you holding the camera steady?
- Are the horizontals and verticals straight?
- If you are standing 3-6 ft (1-2 m) from your subject, have you allowed for parallax?

If the shutter won't press, don't panic! It could be for one of the following reasons:

There is no film in the camera

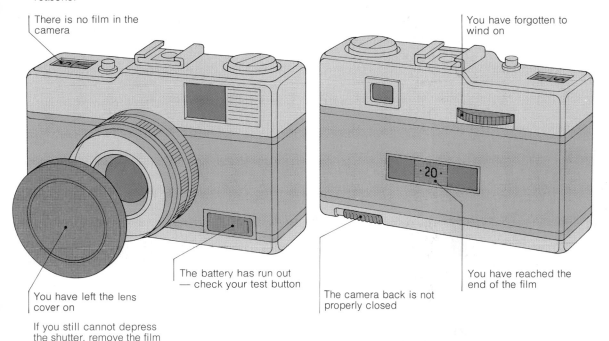

You have forgotten to wind on

You have left the lens cover on

The battery has run out — check your test button

The camera back is not properly closed

You have reached the end of the film

If you still cannot depress the shutter, remove the film and take the camera to be repaired.

Camera and lens care

Your camera is a precision-made instrument. Take care to protect it from heat, dust, sand and water. A case will cushion the camera against knocks and enable you to carry it in a pocket or bag. Never leave your camera in a hot place, such as the glove pocket or back shelf of an automobile. Beware of water and fine sand at the beach; keep the camera in a waterproof bag. If you do get water or sand in the camera, have it cleaned by an expert. Remove the batteries when storing

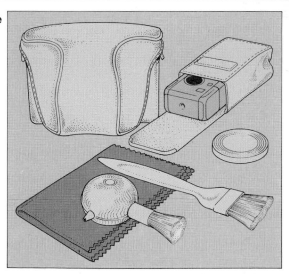

the camera for a long time, to prevent possible leakage. You should protect your lens from scratches, fingermarks, moisture, dust and intense sunlight. Always keep the lens cap or a skylight filter over the lens when you are not using the camera. If you want to clean the lens, remove the dust first with a camel hair brush or, better still, a puffer brush. Then wipe over the lens gently with an antistatic camera lens cloth. *Never* breathe on the lens and wipe it with a handkerchief.

Choosing the best viewpoint

There are endless ways of photographing a subject, inside or out of doors, so before you shoot, move around and examine it from different angles and heights. Notice how the image in your frame is affected. The background changes, and altered perspective influences the subject's shape. Whichever viewpoint you decide on, always make sure that your subject fills the frame.

The most obvious viewpoint of our subject, right, was from the side, at normal height. The result is a straightforward record, but unimaginative and "posed" looking. An oblique view, below, shows more of the horse, but the overall effect of the shot is very similar.

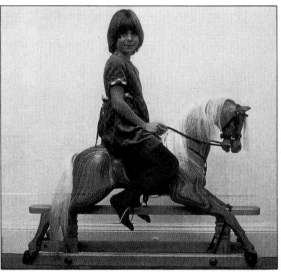

Front view
A head-on view at normal height makes the horse look as though it is little more than a piece of furniture — all its shape is lost.

Low down and high up
A low viewpoint, above, sets the subject against the plain wall, making it look tall and majestic. By contrast, a high viewpoint, right, makes the horse merge with the wooden floor and the overall effect is distorted.

Special qualities

A good choice of viewpoint will help you achieve a good result, but you must be imaginative in order to get some really special shots. The photographer took this charming shot, right, from the horse's tail and asked the child to twist around in her seat. A low viewpoint, close in, far right, makes the horse seem larger and more powerful in relation to the child — the shot has a lively quality which the others lack.

Close-ups

You may find, even after you have moved around the subject and examined it from different angles, that you cannot clear a muddled background. Instead of attempting to show the whole subject, try moving right in close, as above, and concentrating on one part only. You can then get rid of intrusive background elements.

Some common faults

When composing your pictures, beware of making the following basic mistakes:

- There may be other objects that you want to include in the shot, but be careful how you arrange them. It is usually better to keep the background as uncluttered as you possibly can.

- The plant may be an attractive addition to the shot, but it shouldn't look as though it is growing straight out of the subject's head.

- Watch your framing. Make sure that your shot is not spoiled by distracting objects around the edges of the frame.

Framing for strong pictures

Careful framing can create a striking, well-composed picture from a simple scene, like the one above. The off-center position of the house is strong and dynamic, while the low horizon emphasizes the dramatic sky. The picture uses the "rule of thirds", shown right. Imagine lines dividing your frame into thirds. Position your main subject at one of the four intersections and let the lines suggest divisions of the frame. A centered subject often looks static, while a central horizon tends to split a picture in two.

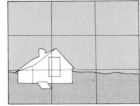

Balance
A shot composed of objects of the same color, size or shape may look repetitive and dull. You will create a livelier effect by balancing dissimilar objects. The shot right balances horizontal against vertical, bright color against neutral tone.

Line to emphasize mood

Many subjects have a predominance of one kind of line — horizontal, vertical or diagonal. Each of these conveys a special mood, which you can exploit by careful framing. Horizontal lines, below, convey balance and calm. Vertical lines suggest height and grandeur, as in the tele shot right. Diagonal lines, far right, are restless and dynamic. If your viewfinder is rectangular, let the dominant lines of your subject dictate whether you choose to frame the picture horizontally or vertically.

Using the foreground

If you leave the foreground empty, your shot is likely to be flat and dull. Don't waste space — use the foreground to create depth or emphasis in your pictures. A foreground frame will draw the eye into the picture and focus attention on the main subject. Try shooting through an arch or window, left, or improvise by using low-hanging foliage to frame your shot.

Line to suggest depth

You can also use line to suggest depth if you choose the right viewpoint. In the picture right, the curve of the railway line links the foreground to the background, leading the eye into the scene. An oblique viewpoint has exaggerated the curve, adding rhythm to the picture. The parallel lines of the pier, far right, appear to converge as they recede. The perspective effect is strengthened by the low camera viewpoint. A high viewpoint would have foreshortened the pier and reduced the sense of depth.

Making use of natural light

Light is perpetually changing — in color, direction and quality. And in changing, it alters the appearance of the world around us. Different subjects call for different kinds of lighting. You must learn to recognize the kind of light that will enhance the qualities and mood of your particular subject. Often it is just a question of noticing and using natural light as it occurs. Sometimes you can exploit and improve it by moving around your subject (see facing page).

Time of day
Between sunrise and sunset, daylight presents a range of colors and moods. At dawn, top left, colors are muted and outlines softened. By mid-morning, top right, the sun is high in the sky, casting hard-edged shadows. The early afternoon sun, center, brings out strong color and detail. By late afternoon the sun is starting to set, below left, bathing the scene in a golden light, while dusk, below, creates a cool, mysterious mood.

The direction of light

As the sun moves across the sky, it strikes the earth from different angles. At noon, you must be content with overhead lighting. At other times of day you can alter the angle of the light by moving around your subject.

Side-lighting, below left, reveals the texture and form of the tide-mill, where back-lighting, below, throws the building into dramatic silhouette, suppressing all color and detail. Front-lighting, right, flattens both form and texture but enhances color.

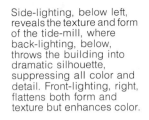

The quality of light

Light may be either soft or hard, depending on weather and time of day. When the sun is filtered by cloud, mist or rain, it gives soft, even lighting which mutes color and brings out detail, above. When the sun is bright and direct, shining from overhead or behind the camera, it gives hard, frontal lighting with sharp-edged shadows, left. Storms can produce dramatic colors and shafts of light, right.

Making use of flash

Flash enables you to take photographs at any time, no matter how dim the lighting. You can use it both indoors and out to supplement existing light, brighten colors, fill in shadows or freeze action (p.36). Its one drawback is that you cannot see its effect in advance — you must learn to predict where its shadows will fall. Always make sure that your main subject lies well within the flash range. You can use flash fall-off (p.23) to clear a cluttered background. Just move the subject away from the background and let flash fall-off darken it. Try using flash to light up a dim interior, like the bar room right. Leave room lights switched on to add a realistic touch.

Flash or available light?
Flash has enriched colors and illuminated background detail in the picture above left, but the girl has a lifeless, glazed expression. When taking portraits, you will create a more natural effect if you soften the flash (see facing page) or ask people not to look directly at it, as in the top shot. When flash is not used, above, the whole scene looks darker, colors are duller and shadowy detail is lost. But shooting by available light has recorded more of the atmosphere of the bar.

Flash for bright color
Toward the end of the day or when the sky is overcast, there is not enough light to do justice to the colors and details of a small object, like the plaque, left. So use flash to simulate sunlight and brighten colors, as in the picture above.

Creating softer lighting

Flash is a fairly hard, directional light source that can cast ugly shadows. You can create softer, more even lighting by diffusing it. Cover the flash head with one layer of white handkerchief, as below, or use a ready-made diffuser.

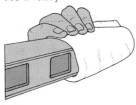

Alternatively, if you can tilt your flash unit or use it off camera, try bouncing the light off a white wall or ceiling, as shown below.

Flash portraits

Direct on-camera flash has produced a flat, two-dimensional portrait and thrown sharp-edged shadows behind the two figures, above. Diffusing the flash minimizes the back shadows and adds depth to the picture right. Detail is now revealed in shadow areas, such as the folds of the man's jacket. Always diffuse flash when working close up.

Using fill-in flash

When the sun casts dark shadows, you can use flash to lighten or "fill in" shadow areas. Position your flash on the other side of your subject to the sun, so as to throw light on areas of densest shadow. Dark shadows are a common problem when you take portraits by a window or in harsh midday sunlight. In the picture above left back-lighting has obscured the face with shadow while rimming the head with a halo of light. Fill-in flash gives more detail in the face but retains the halo, above.

Flash faults

"Red eye" is seen in close-ups of people and animals when on-camera flash has been used at subject eye-level. It is most pronounced when available light is very dim and the iris of the eye is wide open. If you cannot use flash off camera, either diffuse it or increase room lighting. And make sure your subject is not looking straight at the camera. On-camera flash may also produce intrusive flare spots if you shoot facing a mirror, window or other reflective surface. Shooting from an oblique angle is the best way to avoid reflections.

Taking pictures at night

You can take some pictures at night even with a simple camera if you use 400 ASA film.

Try shooting light sources for their own sake, filling the frame with light and color. Or concentrate on subjects that are well lit — either artificially or by the last light of day. Dusk is a good time to shoot night photographs — the dark blue sky combined with the effect of house and street lights gives an impression of night, and there is still enough light to record form and shadow detail, right. The shots on this page were taken hand-held, without long exposure (see chart on facing page). Avoid camera shake by supporting the camera.

Colored lights
Street lights and neon signs make colorful subjects. Fill the frame with sharp pinpoints of light, above. Or use your closest focusing setting to blur the light sources and create an abstract pattern of light circles and trails, right.

Brightly lit areas
You can take any subject at night, without a long exposure, if it is lit brightly enough. Shopping centers, store windows and cinema or theater entrances provide a bright, even spill of light. To photograph a person at night, stand your subject close to the light source so that the face is well lit, above. Shooting after rain when sidewalks are wet and reflective will help to light up a dark foreground.

More advanced cameras allow longer exposures (1/15 to 1 sec or more) or manual time exposures, opening up a far wider range of night shots.

Automobile lights, fireworks, even the moon will trace patterns of light across the frame during a long exposure, right. If you move the camera smoothly while the shutter is open, you can also create interesting light patterns with static light sources. Plan your movement to get a pleasing pattern, below. Always use a tripod when taking long exposures. For manual time exposures use the B setting — the shutter stays open as long as the release is depressed.

Bracketing exposure

At night the range of light is too contrasty for your exposure meter to judge accurately. In addition, film reacts unpredictably to long exposures. The chart, right, gives approximate exposure times. But to be sure of results you must take two or three shots, doubling or halving the initial exposure each time. This is called "bracketing". The picture right (exposed for two seconds), the best shot of a set of three, shows a good balance of shadow detail and highlights. The longer exposure recorded more detail in the shadows, but "burnt out" the lights. The shorter exposure was too dark. It makes sense to bracket whenever lighting conditions are uncertain.

Exposure times

This chart shows the shutter speeds suggested with 400 ASA color film for a variety of subjects. It assumes a wide aperture (f2.8) except for the starred items (f16). Find out from your camera manual which night shots you can take.

Dusk shots	1/60 sec
Store windows	1/60 sec
Theater entrances	1/60 sec
Neon signs	1/60 sec
Well-lit street	1/30 sec
Portrait by bonfire	1/30 sec
Street lights	1/15 sec
City panorama	1/15 sec
Campfires	1/15 sec
Floodlit buildings	1/8 sec
Candlelight	1/4 sec
Auto light trails*	1/2 sec
Fireworks*	1 sec
Full moon landscape	1-5 mins
Moon and star trails*	20 mins

Handling action shots

Shots of moving subjects require careful planning, whether you want to freeze the action, or let it blur to suggest speed.

Flash will stop all blur, as shown right, if your subject is in range and lighting is dim. Without flash, shutter speed is important — the hands below are blurred at 1/30 sec, sharp at 1/125 sec. With an automatic camera you will get faster speeds in bright light, so you can freeze action, and slower speeds in dim light, so it will blur. Plan your viewpoint in advance — it is easier to stop action if it is moving toward you, or at its peak, see below. Using a low viewpoint often helps to clear a distracting background.

Peak of action
Action often slows, or even halts, at its peak — the top of a leap, for instance, or the height of a swing, as right. Such moments make dramatic shots, and are easier to freeze. Choose a viewpoint that will enable you to catch the peak of action against a clear background. Prefocus on the point where you expect the action to occur, and wait for the right moment to press the shutter.

Panning for fast action
To "pan" the camera, focus on a point that the subject will pass. Swing your whole body smoothly to keep the subject in the finder, as shown right, and press the shutter when it reaches the point you have selected. Practice before shooting.

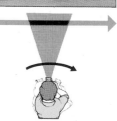

Shoot head-on

You can freeze action most easily if you shoot it either head-on, as with the circus horse below, or moving directly away from you. Action shots from the side, are much more likely to show blur, as the shot right shows.

Using a slow shutter

Where part of a scene is moving and part still, you can get effective shots at slow speeds. A blurred arch frames a jostling crowd, above (hand held, 1/8 sec). Headlamps make trails behind a sharp silhouette, right (tripod, 5 secs).

Suggesting speed

You can make slow action, above, much more dramatic by "overpanning' and using diagonal lines (p.29) in your composition, as right. Start your pan from just *behind* the subject and pan smoothly past it to blur subject and background.

Using color effectively

Strong color is vibrant and bold. Only bright, direct lighting will bring out its full brilliance.

Color is the single most powerful element in any picture; so you should control it carefully. Generally, a restricted color range is more effective than a mass of unrelated colors. The shot of the bus, right, is bright and colorful without being gaudy — strong colors are well balanced by more neutral tones. Taking a detail from the bus picture, below, strengthens color contrast and simplifies the composition. You will achieve the most dynamic color contrast if you offset warm colors with cold ones.

Finding isolated color
Even a relatively small area of strong color will dominate a picture when set against a neutral or monochromatic background, right. When the sky is overcast and dull, the sea gray and stormy, or the scene drab, look out for chance occurrences of isolated color.

Color for color's sake
Moving in close to the striped canvas chairs, above, has created a bold, semi-abstract picture, using color for color's sake. The effect is enriched by back-lighting. Multiple color contrast requires careful handling — keep the composition as simple as possible, and frame your subject tightly in order to exclude any weaker color elements.

Muted color can be romantic, bleak or dramatic. Soft lighting brings out its subtle range of tones.

In the shaded street scene, right, diffused lighting has softened and merged colors and shapes. Even the bright blue stripes of the towel appear subdued. Look for muted colors when light is scattered by haze, rain or smoke.

Harmony in nature
You can convey a feeling of harmony by restricting your view to a range of tones of one particular color, as above, or a variety of pastel shades. Nature provides an ideal source of inspiration for harmonious color pictures. In the tranquil landscape above, the repetition of the shapes of the trees adds greatly to the harmony of the composition.

Shooting in black and white

Black and white is graphic or abstract, where color is sensual and realistic. Use it to bring out texture, to simplify lines and shapes, or to provide atmosphere.

The main advantage of black and white is its simplicity. A subject that is overwhelmed by a mass of colors will look much more powerful when reproduced in black and white. Try using its subtle range of tones to suggest texture, right. Indirect light or side-lighting will enhance the textural effect (p.31). Or choose it when you want to emphasize a strong shape. Frame your subject against a background of contrasting tone for additional impact, as below. A sharp black/white contrast of highlights and dense shadows makes a strikingly dramatic picture, below right.

Coping with dim light

Fast black and white film is the best choice for dimly lit interiors, such as the bar room right. It allows brief exposure, effectively freezing movement. The grainy quality of the film adds atmosphere. If color had been used the busy background might have distracted attention away from the people and the mixed lighting would have caused a color cast (p. 15).

Uprating the film

If lighting is very poor, you can obtain even higher film speeds in black and white by "uprating" or "pushing" the film. Set the ASA dial at up to three times the proper film speed and remember to tell the laboratory, so that they can give extra processing to your film. You can also uprate color slide film to a limited extent.

Manipulating your print

Black and white film is both easier and cheaper to manipulate in the darkroom. There are various ways in which your negatives can be printed to create a special effect. They can be sepia-toned, trimmed ("cropped") to give a stronger composition or printed in a faded-out ("vignetted") oval. Or ask your processor to modify the range of tones to create a predominantly dark and dramatic (low-key) or light, romantic (high-key) print.

Creating a high-key mood

The soft, delicate tones of the portrait right were produced in the darkroom. The unmodified original is shown above. If you want to achieve a high-key effect, choose a basically light-toned subject and use soft, indirect lighting so as to avoid creating harsh shadows.

The family at home

The pictures you take of your family at home are likely to be among your most successful — you are working with people and surroundings that you know well and your camera is always at hand when an exciting picture-taking opportunity arises. Don't allow your familiarity with your home to blind you to distracting colors and details in the background. Try to avoid highly patterned wallpaper and furnishings in the house and brightly colored flowers and shrubs outside. Whenever possible, use natural light indoors and soft, diffused sunlight outside. When shooting a group of people, right, try to pose them around a center of interest (p.58).

Choosing the moment
Timing is as important as any technical skill when taking pictures of people. Wait until faces and gestures are animated, as above, then shoot quickly. Don't economize on film — it may take several shots to get a lively composition.

Capturing expressions
A child's quieter moments can be just as revealing as her livelier moods, as right. Use a tele lens or move in close to catch these characteristic expressions. Remember to compensate for parallax when focusing close-ups (p.18).

Double portraits

When photographing two people, try to express the relationship between them. Shoot when they are looking at each other, as below, or in the same direction, far right. The picture will lack unity if they are looking in opposite directions, right.

Unobserved shots

You will achieve the most natural, unselfconscious pictures of your family when they are unaware of the camera. Shoot while they are absorbed in an activity, selecting a viewpoint that shows clearly what they are doing. Children look most natural when photographed from their own eye level. Notice how back-lighting from the window has muted colors and provided a soft frame for the children painting, right. All the shots on these pages were taken in natural light. If your camera can't cope, use diffused flash (p.33).

Babies – the early months

Owning a camera gives you the unique opportunity to make a visual diary of your baby's development. During his first year, a baby learns to master many new skills—from feeding himself to taking his first steps—so take pictures regularly. Whenever possible, use natural lighting indoors and soft, even lighting outside. If flash is necessary, diffuse or bounce it—direct on-camera flash is too harsh. Don't pose your baby or dress him up specially for the occasion. Get down to his level and photograph him among his toys in familiar surroundings. A very young baby will feel most relaxed and secure when cradled in his mother's arms, as right.

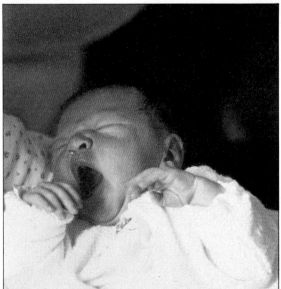

Propping up your baby
Until a baby is strong enough to sit up on his own, you will have to find some means of support. The best way is to use soft-toned cushions or a pillow—the mother's arm in the picture right is intrusive. A change of viewpoint would have hidden it behind the baby.

Expressive moments
Babies make delightfully unselfconscious subjects for photography. Make the most of their fascinating range of expressions by having your camera ready at all times. Sometimes you can use a toy or rattle to attract a baby's attention. A quick reaction to the situation was required to capture the baby in mid-yawn, left.

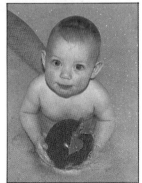

Moving in close
A close viewpoint has blurred the grass in the foreground and isolated the baby, emphasizing her growing self-awareness. The hazy blue sky provides a soft background. When taking close-ups, be sure to allow for parallax (p.18).

44

Children growing up

Children can be lively and excited one moment, quiet and pensive the next. Make the most of their ever-changing moods and expressions by taking your camera with you on all occasions.

Ready-made situations
You will capture children at their most spontaneous when their attention is absorbed. Outings often provide tailor-made opportunities for candid shots. For the picture below, the photographer waited until expressions were animated and interesting before shooting.

Common errors
Both the pictures left are ruined by self-consciousness. The boys are acting up to the camera while the pair below are already bored by being photographed. You can avoid results like this by giving children something absorbing to do.

Unusual viewpoints
An unusual viewpoint often helps you take pictures without being seen—giving you time to consider composition. In the shot below notice how the girl's leg and boy's arm create a pleasing sense of balance.

Coping with a shy child
If a child is shy of the camera, try to put him at ease by turning the whole occasion into a game. Let him take your picture instead, or join in a game of peek-a-boo, as in the picture left.

Using light and color

You can greatly enhance the mood of your shots by using color and lighting sensitively. Back-lighting adds a bright, sunny mood to the picture of the little girl, below, caught in a high-spirited moment. The somber background tone and dull lighting contribute to the thoughtful mood of the boy, below right. The brilliant yellow of the balloon makes a dramatic contrast with clothing and background colors. The dreamy, slightly wistful mood of the little boy at the window, right, is enhanced by soft lighting and harmonious tones.

Capturing children at play

A group of children involved in play will soon forget the camera, enabling you to shoot freely. Be patient and wait until an interesting situation develops, then shoot fast before the moment is lost. The diagram below shows what might have happened if the photographer had not reacted quickly. The seashore provides children with an endless source of fascination. Get down to their own level for the most natural-looking shots. Remember that back views can sometimes be just as expressive as front views.

Portraits by natural light

Taking good portraits is not always easy, but a combination of time, care and patience will give you excellent results. If you follow the guidelines on these pages, you will avoid the commonest pitfalls. First, choose a fairly close viewpoint, say 4-5 ft (1.2-1.5 m), so that your subject dominates the frame (p.19). Then study him from different sides. Few people have such regular features that they look good from any angle. A three-quarter view, right, generally seems the most natural. Choose a plain background, taking into account coloring and clothing. If the background is cluttered, move your sitter away from it, or use close focusing (p. 19). Never allow the background to dominate, as below right. Lastly, check your framing for parallax (p.18) and make sure exposure is right for the face itself (p.20).

Capturing personality
Many people become self-conscious in front of a camera—much depends on your ability to relax the sitter, so that he forgets the camera. If you want to capture an animated expression, keep your sitter talking while you shoot. Include hands if they help to reveal character, as above. Or shoot while the sitter is absorbed in an activity, as left, to capture a more serious side of his personality. Never ask your subject to stand still and look into the lens—the result will be stiff and unflattering, as right.

Using light outdoors

Strong overhead sunlight can make people squint and may cast shadows beneath the eyes, nose and chin, below left. You can usually create a more flattering effect by turning your sitter's head until the face is in light shadow and the sun highlights the hair, below right. Hazy or cloudy days, right, provide the best lighting conditions. The soft, diffused light produces good facial modeling and your subject can look comfortably at the camera, no matter how high the sun is in the sky.

Using light indoors

When taking indoor portraits, position your sitter about 4 ft (1.2 m) from a window. On a sunny day, the light may be harsh and directional. To soften the lighting and create a more romantic effect, smear a little grease on a filter (or piece of glass) placed over the lens while you shoot, as above (p. 90). Or exploit the dramatic lighting contrast by taking your sitter side-on to the window, right. Use fast film for indoor portraits in order to allow for unpredictable lighting conditions.

Taking good candids

The appeal of candid shots lies in their naturalness and spontaneity. For good pictures, your subjects must be oblivious of the camera. This means shooting either when people are engrossed in some activity, or when you can remain unobtrusive by using an unexpected viewpoint or a tele lens. The expressions and emotions that make a strong candid photograph are fleeting. You will have to work quickly and shoot when the decisive moment occurs. It often helps to preset focus and exposure when you find yourself in a promising location, like a street market or carnival. A quick response to the moment captured the delight of the woman, right, who was watching street theater.

Unusual viewpoints
You can often get closer to your subject without being seen, by choosing an unusual viewpoint. A side view provided an informal shot of a man at work on his boat, above.

Tele shots
Children make excellent candid subjects. Make the most of lively expressions when their attention is absorbed. A tele slide enables you to fill the frame from a distance — the change appears in the viewfinder, as shown left.

Catching the moment
Gestures can be as telling as facial expressions in candid shots. The picture above captured the precise moment when the women's stance and gestures were most expressive. An eye for color and composition strengthens the shot right.

Hobbies and work

A friend with an interesting hobby or job makes a good subject for informal shots. Your main aim should be to link the person closely with his activity so that they make an integrated subject.

If you choose an intricate hobby like model-making, you will want to bring out detail and color, so use flash to supplement daylight. Move in close to show exactly what your subject is doing and frame your shots tightly. Exclude from your picture anything that is not associated with the activity — a neutral background is best. Above all, try to convey the skill and concentration demanded by the hobby — show your subject looking at his work, not the camera.

Choosing viewpoint
Study your subject from many different angles. An eye-level viewpoint, top, gives a good overall view of both man and boat. But you may have to use a low viewpoint to capture expressions, as far left, because people lower their heads when working with their hands. A high viewpoint, left, emphasizes the hobby's precision. (See the camera positions above.)

Capturing atmosphere

Photographing a person in his working environment demands a slightly different approach. Here it is more important to capture atmosphere than detail, so use natural light and fast film and shoot when your subject is close to a bright light source, such as the forge fire. Try to leave your subject undisturbed — otherwise your pictures will be stiff and artificial. Look out for characteristic actions and postures that express the nature of your subject's occupation. For the picture right the photographer stepped back to show the blacksmith framed by the tools of his trade. Grease was used to harmonize colors and soften the lighting (p. 90).

Camera angles

A low camera angle, below, has captured the blacksmith's jovial personality and you can almost feel the heat from the furnace. Move in to your closest focusing distance to shoot details, as in the bottom shot.

Freezing movement

400 ASA film will allow you to freeze motion, even in low lighting conditions, giving a realistic flavor to your pictures. Notice how the angle of the flying sparks adds dynamism to the picture right (p. 29).

Photographing your possessions

When you photograph a treasured possession, take your time to light and arrange it properly.

If it is a large object such as an automobile, motorbike or boat, decide which feature or quality you want to bring out. Strong light will make the most of bright colors and reflective surfaces, as right. The low, three-quarter view exaggerates the size of the hood and front wheels. A higher viewpoint from the side, coupled with the dominant horizontals in the background, emphasizes the sleek, low lines of the car below. A greased filter makes highlights sparkle, below right. A cross-screen filter has the same effect (p.90).

Focusing on detail
You must get right in close to pick out a characteristic detail, such as the insignia, left. A close-up lens is a useful accessory (p.82). Frame your subject so that lines, shapes and colors make an interesting pattern in the frame.

Photographing a room

When shooting a room interior, you can control your subject as you wish. You can rearrange furniture, change the lighting by partially drawing blinds or curtains, or using lamps (remember that lamps may cause yellow casts, p.15). Don't attempt to record the whole room — concentrate on an attractive corner or wall, as right, keeping the foreground clear. Make sure that verticals line up with the sides of your frame.

Choosing a setting

You may have to move a piece of furniture to show it at its best. In its normal setting, the chair's outline is obscured by other objects, below left. Placing it by a plain wall makes the most of its shape, below right.

Shooting a painting

When photographing a painting, in a gallery or at home, beware of reflections — either of your own image or from a window on the opposite wall, as right. You can exclude reflections, as far right, either by moving the painting to another wall or by shooting from a slight angle, rather than from straight on. Getting someone else to hold a black card behind the camera will also help to minimize any reflections in the glass.

Shooting from above

If you want to show the contents of a display case or workbox, as above, photograph it from directly above and use your closest focusing distance or a close-up lens attachment. Rearrange the box's contents if necessary to make an interesting composition of colors, shapes and textures. And make sure that lighting is even and shadowless. If the light is bright enough, use slow film, as this will show fine detail sharply.

Photographing your pet

Pets, like children, are challenging subjects. To get good results, you require patience, quick reflexes and an understanding of your pet's personality. Use your ingenuity to attract and hold a pet's attention; animals soon lose interest — a strange noise will make a dog prick up his ears, a bowl of food will keep him occupied. Try taking a close-up portrait to show your pet's markings and expressions, as right. If possible, use natural light and a viewpoint that catches the highlights in the animal's eyes.

Anticipate the action
If your dog is bounding along, below, anticipate his likely path and preset focus and exposure. In bright light you should be able to freeze motion as he runs past the camera. In dim light, have the dog run toward you (p.37).

Selecting viewpoint
Photographing a pet from above foreshortens the body and makes the head appear disproportionately large, as above left. Get down to the animal's own level by kneeling or lying on the ground to show its true proportions, as above right.

Play sequence
You will capture the greatest range of poses and expressions if you take your pet playing. Ask a friend to dangle a ball of wool and shoot a sequence in quick succession. Try to keep the same viewpoint.

Small pets
Hamsters, mice and other small pets tend to dart out of range unless securely held, as below.

Shooting aquarium life
Set your camera on a tripod, with the lens against the glass front. To eliminate reflections, fix a piece of black card in front of the camera, with a hole for the lens and viewfinder. A second piece of card on the back of the tank provides a plain background. Insert a glass partition in the tank, to confine the fish and aid focusing. To light the tank, you can either use a spotlight, as in the diagram, or off-camera flash, held above the water. Flash will freeze motion, bring out color, and isolate the fish from its background surroundings, as in the picture right. Never use frontal flash (p.33).

Daytrips and outings

Pictures taken on daytrips and outings form a unique record — you can't go back for more. Take plenty of film (including fast film and flash if the event is likely to run into the evening) and check that your camera is working, and has its case and strap. Try to build a picture story of the whole day. Candid shots of the trip out and back, people you know relaxing together, and humorous incidents are as important as romantic views of the setting. Make sure you have pictures of each occurrence, and of everyone present, yourself included (p.70). These shots were taken on a river picnic. The view from the landing stage, right, sets the scene — the lazy atmosphere and milling pattern of boats.

Arranging group shots
When you take shots of a group of people, your pictures will be stronger if you use part of the setting to provide a frame, as above. The line of the boat links the figures together, as shown left. Alternatively, you can arrange people around a center of interest, as in the picnic shot, above. The figures form a semicircle around the hamper, as shown right. Try to get heads at different levels, to provide variety, and all the faces visible. Then wait for people to relax again before shooting.

People in a setting

You may have to leave the group to get good pictures of them in relation to the setting. Look out for the chance of an unusual viewpoint to help you. The picture on the right was taken from a bridge as the boat passed under it. The overhead view has produced a striking composition. The figures are again framed by the outline of the boat, which links them together. But here their relaxed enjoyment is set in the context of the calm water and cool, harmonious blues and greens of the river (p.39). Individual faces become less important than the atmosphere of the shot. Notice how the small patch of red enlivens the picture.

Capturing humor

The shot above, taken from the bank, shows perfect timing. If there is a lot happening, have your focus and exposure preset, and wait, looking through the viewfinder, for the action to take place — otherwise you will miss it.

Special occasions indoors

When photographing one-off family events, such as a children's Christmas party, try to shoot as many different aspects of the scene as you can. Things happen quickly and children don't stay still for long, so be prepared to shoot fast. Go for the natural effect of a mixture of room- and candle-lighting, adding as many extra lamps as you can to provide enough light. Only resort to flash if it is really too dark, but remember that your shots will lose a great deal of atmosphere. Use 400 ASA film, and a tripod if necessary. With slides you will get an orange cast, unless you use tungsten type film.

The festive spread
Shoot the laden table, left, before people sit down. Try aiming along it for an interesting low viewpoint.

Shooting candles
Reduce the room light a little, but don't turn it off completely, or the flames will be reduced to pinpoints of light. Choose an oblique angle that will set the flames against a dark background.

Photographing groups
When people have sat down, set up your camera. Pay attention to grouping (p.58), making sure that everyone can be seen — particularly small children. Before pressing the shutter, attract everyone's attention and try to make them smile, right. If you take people unawares, results may be disappointing, as above. Candids are more likely to be successful if you concentrate on individuals rather than groups.

Humorous portraits
Take shots of individuals and pairs of people while they are eating and drinking, below. If they are pulling crackers, right, be ready. Act fast to catch expressions. Use simple backgrounds if you possibly can.

Blur for effect
You can add atmosphere to a shot of children opening presents just by allowing subject blur when using a slow shutter speed (p.37) as above. The result gives a feel of flurry and excitement. The shot left is contrived by contrast.

The lit-up tree
Try out different lighting when shooting a group around the tree. Room lights, above, will give you detail; but you will gain atmosphere by relying on the tree lights, above right,

using a slow shutter speed and tripod. (Only the faces closest to the tree will be well lit.) Or try some shots from outside, right. The dark background shows off the lights much better than a light one.

Recording a wedding

Weddings are unrepeatable events, so make sure your camera is working properly and take plenty of film. Don't attempt to cover all aspects of a wedding — concentrate on capturing the mood of the occasion, and leave the traditional poses to the professional. If you try to tackle the more formal shots, you may well get pictures like those right. The group shot is badly organized and mistimed. In the church shot, flash has dazzled the groom and created a harsh light. If possible, try to use available light, below right.

Final preparations
Sunlight streaming through a window has sidelit the group above, delicately modeling their faces. The photographer breathed on a clear filter fixed over the lens in order to soften contrast and enhance the romantic effect (p.90).

Inside the church
If you want to record the ceremony, right, ask first and find a suitable camera position before the service. Here the viewpoint was chosen to include both priest and flowers. Lighting will be dim, so use fast film and a tripod.

The wedding couple

As a friend or relative of the couple, it should be easy for you to obtain some informal portraits. After the ceremony, try to capture the bride and groom in a quiet moment, as below. Wait until they are looking at each other (p.43) and check that their faces are well lit. Or take a picture while they are making a toast, as right. If the reception is held in a marquee you must expect a color cast, but this can be used to effect. Here light shining through the fabric adds a warm glow to the photograph.

At the reception

Move about, looking out for the informal details and incidents that make every wedding unique. Get in close to colorful objects, like the flower basket. Try to get some action shots (p.36) outdoors, where the light is bright enough. Make sure that the background is clear. Vary your viewpoint — get down low to photograph a child, but capture guests decorating the automobile from above.

Recording a show

The brilliant costumes and lighting of stage shows provide a rich range of colorful subjects for photography. All the pictures shown here were taken during a children's production of *The Tempest*. Try to see the show through once before shooting, to make a note of the best moments to record. Shoot some pictures from the wings; others from the auditorium, standing level with, or slightly above, the stage. Take at least one shot of the entire cast, choosing a moment when their grouping is expressive, as in the picture right.

Getting in close
When there are only a few actors on stage, wait for a dramatic point in the action and frame tightly, as above. If you want to capture facial expressions and costume details, right, move in really close or use a tele lens and keep your distance.

Going backstage
Much of the excitement of a stage production happens behind the scenes. So ask permission to go backstage and photograph the cast putting on their makeup or adding the final touches to their costumes. Use flash if you want to brighten colors and show detail, as in the picture above. Beware of getting flash reflections when shooting near mirrors. If you are interested in capturing mood rather than detail, right, use available light—flash tends to destroy atmosphere.

Shooting solo sports

When shooting an individual sport, you should aim not just to show the person but to convey a feeling of their involvement with the sport. You must choose your viewpoint carefully. In the photograph right a side-on shot gives a dramatic profile and a clear view of the pose. The head-on view below shows the whole face but distorts the legs. Don't use flash at subject eye-level (p.33).

Prefocusing
You must prefocus your camera in order to catch fast action. To make sure that the skateboarder was in sharp focus, left, the photographer focused on the red cone and waited for the boy to reach it.

Peak of action
Wait for the action to reach its peak before shooting (p.36), otherwise you may get blur (compare the two shots above). Fluorescent lights may give you a "stroboscopic" effect, as above left.

Using a tele slide

If your camera has a tele lens slide, you will be able to fill the frame quite comfortably from a distance. You will also get near and far parts of the subject in truer proportion. The shot right, if taken from close up with a normal lens, would have shown the horse's head disproportionately large (p.56). If you don't have a tele slide, you will have to move in as close as you can. Rely on your knowledge of the sport and the help of the person you are photographing when planning your shots. Whether you have a tele slide or not, you must be in the right place at the right time and anticipate where the action is going to take place. Always try to get ahead of the action, as right. You can freeze moving subjects more easily if they are moving either toward or away from the camera (p.37). The shot right was taken at 1/250 sec.

Capturing mood

Remember to take some photographs after the action is over, too. The shot above, showing a quiet moment at the end of the day, is a dramatic contrast with the lively activity of the shot on the right.

Shooting team sports

When photographing team sports, aim to convey the special characteristics of the game as well as its energy and excitement. The action is outside your control, so you must choose a good position to shoot from, make use of a tele lens attachment (p.85) to bring the action closer, and wait for the players to pass near by. Knowing the rules of the game will help you to plan and anticipate your shots. Otherwise, watch closely for a while before pressing the shutter. Don't be tempted to shoot when players are in the distance — tiny figures in an expanse of field will convey little of the game. Strong sunlight will help you capture action with fast shutter speeds.

Lighting indoors
If you use flash, as above, you can freeze action (p.36), capture expressions and record color and detail accurately. (Make sure you are within flash range (p.23). Get permission to use flash.) If you rely on available light, top, let a slow shutter blur action to create an abstract effect (p.37). You must sacrifice color and detail, and you may get color cast, but the end result is exciting. Stand at a point where some confrontation will occur. Both shots were taken near the goal.

Isolate the subject
Think about backgrounds and how the participants are grouped. The trees and huddle of players, left, make a confused image. Waiting for two players to pass close by, above, has isolated them against the sky (1/500 sec).

Following a race

When shooting a race, try to record as many different aspects of it as you can. The drama and tension at the start of a swimming race, as the swimmers plunge in, was caught precisely in the shot below. A low, three-quarter viewpoint is best.

Characteristic stances

Study the game closely and pick out the typical actions and stances. Decide what you are aiming for and wait. The tele shot right (1/250 sec) shows the catcher and batter in characteristic attitudes.

During the race, you will have time to follow the swimmers' progress from the edge of the pool. Choose a high viewpoint so that colors and shapes can be clearly seen in the water, as right. Wait for the action to reach its peak (p.36) before shooting — the out-stretched arms and fingers are expressive in this shot.

After the race

At the end, try capturing the participants' triumph and exhaustion. This is also a chance to show faces and portray personalities to contrast with the anonymous figures in the other shots. All three shots were taken with flash.

Going on summer vacation

A vacation by the sea is a favorite time for photography, so make sure you take everything you need. Take with you:

- Plenty of film — fast for night shots; slow if you expect very bright sun
- Flash equipment
- Spare batteries
- Skylight or UV filter (p.90)
- Lens cap
- Lens hood to prevent sunlight causing flare
- Camera case and strap
- Plastic bag to protect equipment on the beach
- At airports keep film in your hand luggage — X-ray security checks can cause film to fog.

Exposure in bright sun
Glare from sand and water may mislead the "eye" of a metering camera into underexposing the main subject, as above. To get subject detail, as above right, either shoot close up and exclude bright areas or shade the "eye" (p.21).

Using a self timer
A self timer enables you to include yourself in a group shot, as shown right. Find a firm camera support and preset focus and exposure. The self timer will fire the shutter about ten seconds after being set, giving you time to join the group.

Shooting on the move
When shooting from a moving vehicle, above, use a fast shutter speed to compensate for vibrations and prevent blur. Hold the camera near (but not touching) the window to avoid reflections and set focus at 15–20ft (5–6.5m).

Recording your trip

Make the most of your vacation by keeping your camera with you at all times. Try to record the key moments and activities of your trip: picnics on the beach, hiking, sunbathing, games on the sand and in the water. Don't forget to take shots of your hotel, or guest house and your favorite restaurant. When taking people in the sea, squat down at the water's edge and keep the camera low. In general, restrict your beach shots to the morning or afternoon. Overhead sun at midday gives short, ugly shadows. Use a skylight filter for all beach pictures if you want to reduce haze. Above all, be imaginative in your approach — turn the camera on fellow photographers or on the family's shadows on a sunlit rock face.

● Always load and unload film in the shade.

Sand, sea and sky

The beach, and elements of sand, sea, sun and sky, whether combined or used separately, make exciting picture-making material. Get to know how to cope with glare off sand and bright water, and how to protect your camera from spray and sand (p.25). A UV filter will also prove to be useful (p.90). Many of your shots will include a horizon; use it to divide up the frame (p.28), and make sure that it is level. When capturing the action of waves breaking, right, get right down low, and use a fast shutter speed (here 1/250 sec). Good results depend on timing.

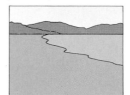

Using reflections
Reflections, whether in wet sand, above, or in water, right, can make the simplest subject into an interesting picture. When photographing perfect mirror-like reflections, make sure that you include all of the reflection.

Beaches
When you are shooting a memorable beach, avoid boring results by getting up high and including some foreground interest. (Compare the shot and diagram above.)

When shooting from the beach, take care over dominant lines. A shot looking out to sea (diagram) would be dull. Shooting along the shoreline produces a lead-in connecting fore- and background.

Light on water

Notice how the direction of sunlight can change the quality of an expanse of water — making it look flat and dull one moment and lively and sparkling the next. Generally, low, oblique light will bring out the textured surface of the water, while light coming from behind you will make it look calm. Back-lighting at dusk, right, has given this stretch of water the appearance of molten metal. Open expanses of water can lack impact — try moving back to include a foreground silhouette, like these palm trees, to give your picture depth and a stronger sense of location. Remember to set exposure for the distant view, not the silhouette.

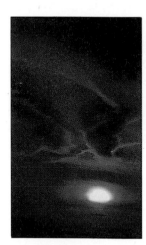

Dramatic skies

If the sky is as striking and colorful as this, above, you need not attempt to introduce any other elements. The shot will be strong enough without. Skies are usually at their most colorful about one hour before sunset.

Capturing local color

A vacation in a foreign country is the perfect time to take pictures. You will see colors, shapes, textures, objects and people with completely fresh eyes, and a whole new range of picture-making material will present itself. Try to take a wide range of different shots which will convey the atmosphere and "feel" of the place to family and friends at home. The general view of a Greek island town, right, is the right kind of scene-setting picture to start your series. It was taken just before dusk.

Choose a theme
If a place has a predominant occupation, such as fishing, take this as a theme and aim for a variety of different shots working around it. A fisherman, above, busy at work provides a chance for a candid tele shot (p.50).

Finding details
Look around for details that convey the essence of your theme: go for images that are rich in color, texture and shape. Rather than trying to shoot the entire boat, above, the photographer picked out the lettering on the bows. Including more in the shot would have made it confusing and muddled. The octopus motif, left, was found on a wall of a house in the town. The close-up of bright yellow nets on the quayside, above, makes an interesting still life composition containing a mass of detail and pattern.

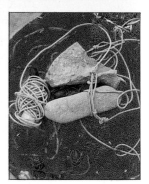

Street color

When you are walking around the streets, look for interesting shops displaying local arts and crafts, right. Remember to move in close to fill the frame with color (p.27). The figure here adds atmosphere and scale.

Local faces

Your collection of shots will come alive if you include some portraits (p.48) of local people. Good results will depend on a friendly approach and a respect for people's feelings, privacy and customs.

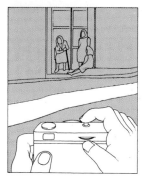

Exposure problems

Taking pictures in bright sun and shade in narrow, white-washed streets can cause exposure problems. With an automatic camera the main thing to remember is to make sure that both you and your subject are in the same kind of lighting (p.21).

The tele shot above left is exposed correctly because subject and photographer were both in shade, as shown in the diagram. With a non-metering camera, set exposure for *subject* lighting.

Time of day

Make the most of the effects of light at different times of day (p.30). Dusk light throws the buildings into dramatic silhouette, above, while mid-morning sun, left, creates hard shadows, giving a strong three-dimensional effect.

Visiting a city

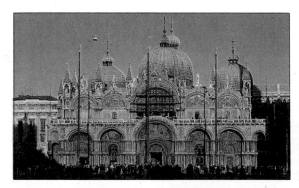

A stay in a strange city gives an ideal chance to photograph buildings. Don't be content with the traditional view of a famous site — study it from all sides (p.26). A shot from one corner, above left, gives a strong sense of perspective, while an entirely different view was obtained from a higher viewpoint, center. Consider light at various times of day, as well as different weather conditions (pp.30-31). Early morning sun adds a golden glow to a head-on view, top, while reflections enliven the foreground of a more distant shot, top right.

High ceilings
Many ornate ceilings in large interiors are lit by high windows. Use fast, daylight film and support the camera when not using flash.

People and views
Putting a member of your family into a shot of a famous place is a perfect way of recording a vacation. If you intend the place itself to be the main subject, don't allow the person to dominate the picture, top right, but put her to one side of the frame, farther away from the camera, bottom right. Having a person look at the building, rather than into the lens, helps to draw attention to the main point of interest.

Mood and atmosphere
Look around for strong, simple images that will evoke memories of the city. (All the shots on these pages were taken in Venice.) The gondolier, right, makes a distinctive shape against the light sky. The shot was taken in early evening when the figure was backlit by low sun (p.31).

Foreground frames
Use arches, bridges and doorways to provide interesting frames for your shots (p.29). Make sure your camera's eye reads for the scene and not for the frame (p.21).

Making a panorama
Use either print or slide film (to be made into prints) to shoot a view that is too wide to fit the frame. Stand in one spot and take about four shots. Use verticals and horizontals as guides and overlap each by about one-third.

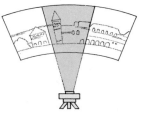

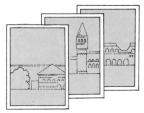

Arrange the finished prints in the correct order. Trim off overlapping areas (if any). Link up the connecting verticals and horizontals in the pictures and stick the completed panorama in your album.

Going on winter vacation

Winter vacations offer a wealth of spectacular and colorful picture ideas. Aim to cover all aspects of your trip — your chalet or hotel; the village (maybe taken from a ski-lift); the evening entertainments; sports shots and dramatic snowscapes. And don't forget to capture the paraphernalia of skiing — skis propped against a fence create a bright abstract pattern, right. In general, stick to close-ups and mid-distance shots — distance and scale are hard to convey in snow unless you include a point of reference, such as a building, in the foreground. Finally, protect your camera by keeping it in its case and carrying it by its strap inside your jacket.

Portraits in snow
Take portraits of people in their ski outfits. Get in close to exclude snow, as above, for correct exposure (p. 70). If snow is included, read exposure from your hand (if your camera allows), not from the snow, to prevent underexposure.

Warm colors for contrast
Enliven your snow shots and balance their dominant cold tones by including warm reds and yellows in the picture, as above. Or shoot at the beginning or end of the day when the snow picks up the warm, golden hues of the sky.

UV filter
Sunlit snow scenes often turn out looking blue rather than white because the blue of the sky is reflected in shadow areas, as shown left, and ultra violet light is present at high altitudes. A UV filter helps reduce excess blue, above.

Capture people in action

Include some dynamic shots of people skiing among your vacation pictures. Even with a simple camera you will be able to get a reasonably sharp result if you preset focus and exposure for a given spot in the skier's path and pan the camera as he approaches the point of focus (p.36). Keep down low in order to frame the skier against the sky.

Lighting snow

To bring out the crisp texture and sparkling brilliance of snow, use low side- or back-lighting, as shown below. Snow looks dull and flat when photographed in overcast conditions or with the sun behind the camera.

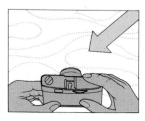

Focus on a detail

Close-ups of frosty leaves or thick blankets of snow on roofs or fences often evoke the icy feeling of winter better than distant snow scenes. Set them against a dark background and use side-lighting to reveal texture, as right.

Landscapes and views

Strong landscapes result from an appreciation of the effects of light, weather and season and a talent for conveying distance. Don't put your camera away when weather seems uninviting. Mist and haze will mute colors and create a sense of mystery. Storms produce dramatic light changes — low clouds sweep across the sky, dappling the land with dense shadows and brilliant highlights, as above. To obtain maximum sharpness in a distant view, set focus at 15-20 ft (4.5-6 m). Using the infinity setting will put the foreground out of focus (p.19).

Be selective
Try not to clutter your landscapes with too much detail, as above. Select part of the scene with a strong focal point, as in the tele shot right. And, if the sky is dull or pale, consider excluding it from the picture altogether.

Depth and distance

Landscapes often turn out disappointing — a richly detailed view becomes a featureless green mass on the final print. This is because your picture lacks the illusion of depth. Try to find a way of linking foreground and background. Use undulating or diagonal lines and shapes to draw the eye back, as below and right. Better still, use a strong foreground shape to frame a view and indicate distance by its relative size. Notice how the tree lends balance and tonal contrast to the scene.

Other ways to imply depth

- Shoot parallel lines converging steeply into the distance.
- Use an open gate to frame a view and invite the eye into the picture.
- Include a figure in the foreground, looking at the view, not at you (p.76).

Using direction of light

Decide what is your subject's most striking feature and use lighting and viewpoint to accentuate it. If texture is the main attraction in a scene, don't shoot on overcast days. Wait until you can use the shadows created by low side-lighting to bring it out, as in the picture right. Where shape is dominant, shoot with the sun behind your subject. Expose for the sky and let the foreground shape be reduced to a silhouette. A low viewpoint has exaggerated the height and shape of the wintry tree, left.

Nature in close-up

Most plants and insects are too small to look impressive when shot with a normal lens, even at its closest focusing distance, as shown by the poppy field, far right. To make the most of the colors, textures and intricate patterning of the natural world, you must get nearer to your subject by using a close-up lens. This acts like a magnifying glass, enabling you to fill the frame with a single bloom, like the poppy head, right. When working close up, depth of field (p.19) is very limited, so accurate focusing is vital if you are to ensure that your main subject looks sharp. Use a steel rule to measure the exact camera-to-subject distance advised for your lens. And use your eyes to check that the lens is precisely aligned with your subject — parallax compensation marks are inaccurate when working at such proximity.

Close-up lenses
Some 110s have built-in close-up or "macro" lenses that slide over the normal lens. Close-up lenses for 35 mm cameras, shown below, screw on to the front of the normal lens. They are measured in various strengths or "diopters".

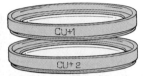

Making a windshield
Staple a sheet of stiff cardboard to two stakes and position it in the wind's path behind the flower, as shown above.

Lighting and movement
Choose soft but fairly bright lighting for close-ups, so that you can use a small aperture and increase depth of field. If available light is dim, use diffused flash, as in the shot of the seed head, right. Flash also helps to overcome the problem of subject motion. When you use a close-up lens, any movement of either camera or subject is magnified and creates blur. A tripod and cable release will eliminate camera shake, but to cope with plants swaying in the wind, you must either use flash or a windshield, as shown left.

Knowing your subject
Successful nature photography depends on being in the right place at the right time. You must be up early to capture the morning dew on a spider's web. Move around until the light is caught in the dewdrops and the web is against a dark background.

Time and patience
Photographing butterflies demands a lot of time and patience. Be as quiet as you can and wait for the insect to settle, preferably on a flower or leaf of contrasting color, as shown below.

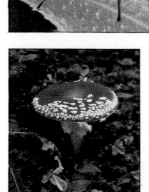

Using back-lighting
The color and shape of translucent plants show up best by strong back-lighting. In soft, diffused light the seed-pod looks dull in color and merges into the background. When backlit by strong sunlight, color is intensified and the pod is outlined by a halo of light.

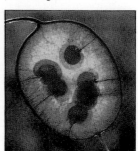

Unexpected color
Mushrooms and toadstools can be as colorful as flowers. Choose a view that reveals their best feature, as shown above and right.

Framing for effect
Be imaginative in your framing, as right. Placing the lily off-center has focused attention on the bright pink flower (p.28).

Zoo animals and birds

Photographing animals in zoos is not easy — they are either too far off, asleep, behind bars, or obscured by shade or ugly settings. A tele lens helps, but timing and viewpoint are just as important. An animal often makes regular trips around its enclosure. Observe it, and pick a spot where it will approach closely, and be in sunlight or set against a contrasting backdrop of grass, leaves or sky. Focus on the spot, and set your exposure for it. Then wait. With large animals try to include something that shows scale, as in the tele shot of the giraffes, above.

Humor and interest
A sequence of action shots in close succession from one viewpoint often conveys the humor of an animal's behavior better than one picture. This pair was busy playing up to the crowd, so the photographer had time for several shots.

Pose and setting

Knowing an animal's habits can help you find it in a characteristic pose, and an attractive setting. Try catching the big cats in the afternoon, when they like to laze and play in the sun. This beautiful leopard was lolling on the roof of its shelter, where a bush made a leafy setting. The shot was taken with a tele lens, which has filled the frame and put the background out of focus, making the animal stand out more clearly.

Avoiding cage bars

Wire netting or bars in the foreground will spoil your pictures, as left. To avoid this, you may be able to arrange your camera so that the lens "sees" between the bars. Alternatively, if you can, choose a wide aperture to narrow depth of field (p.19) and place your camera close to the bars to throw them out of focus, as shown right. Check that shooting through bars is permitted, and is safe.

Using a tele lens

Pocket cameras with a built-in tele lens are very useful for zoo shots. Moving a switch on the camera brings an additional lens over the main one, enlarging the image by 50 to 60 percent. The viewfinder usually shows you this change. A tele lens helps you to fill the frame, as these shots of flamingos show. It also reduces the depth of field so that that background blurs, as in the leopard shot above.

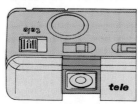

Ordering your prints

There is a wide variety of printing services on the market. The chart, right, shows what the main ones offer and how costs compare. Many services provide a range of surface finishes — the most common are mat, glossy and luster. And most don't charge for any picture that fails to print. The main advantage of the costlier services is that they assess each negative individually, which allows for exposure variation and gives superior quality. And they will enlarge a part of the negative. To order an enlargement from part of the negative only, mask the negative with tracing paper and indicate the exact area you want to have blown up.

Service	How to find it	What it offers	Quality	Cost	Speed
Mail order	Magazine advertisement Postal mailings	Standard print sizes: 3½×3½″ print from 126; 4¼×3½″ from 110 and 5×3½″ from 35 mm	Prints bulk-processed Quality fluctuates Difficult to complain	Cheapest, but credit systems can commit you and/or make it more costly	Usually about one week, depending on mail service
Local photo or drug store	Main street	Same as above	Same variable quality as above, but possible to complain	Cheap	Quick, usually 3–5 days
Amateur photo lab	Photographic magazines	Will print any size from 110, 126 and 35 mm negs. Most provide print-from-slide service	Good quality and service	More costly Economic price-offers for whole-neg enlargement, only ×7	Quick, usually 5 days
Professional lab	Phone book or trade directory	Same as above, but may not do 110 Any feasible enlargement	Very good quality Specialized service	Most expensive, but gives free contacts — you specify enlargements	Very quick, 24 hours or less if required

Choosing a print for enlargement
Among your prints there may be several that you would like to enlarge further. But, to enlarge well, a shot must be very sharp, and you can only judge this from the negative, not from the resulting print.

Both the negatives shown left would give reasonable standard-sized prints. But when part of each negative is enlarged by several times, the difference is obvious. So when choosing a shot, always examine the negative for sharpness with a magnifying glass.

Recognizing faults

Using the camera
- **Subject "bleached out"**
  Don't use direct flash too
  near subject (p.23).
  Diffuse flash when
  working close up (p.33)
- **Camera let in light**
  Make sure camera back
  is properly closed while
  film is in camera (p.11)
- **Film loaded twice**
  When unloading 35 mm
  film, wind film tongue
  back into cassette, or
  clearly mark exposed
  roll of film

Taking the picture
- **Cluttered background**
  Look around frame and
  beyond main subject to
  check background is
  clear of distracting
  objects (p.27)
- **Person squinting**
  For portraits, make sure
  subject is not looking
  directly into sun (p.49)
- **Subject too far away**
  Consider main subject's
  size in relation to frame.
  Exclude anything that
  doesn't contribute to shot

Processing and handling
- **Dust on negative**
  Negatives carelessly
  handled at processors.
  Send film back and
  complain
- **Strong color cast**
  Processor has used
  wrong filtering.
  Send film back and
  complain
- **Film affected by heat**
  Never leave film or
  camera in hot place,
  glove pocket or back
  shelf of automobile (p.25)

Presenting your pictures

If you are pleased with the pictures you have taken, it's worth spending a little time and money on displaying them well.

Building up an album
The ideal way of displaying your prints is in an album. Make the best possible use of the page and try to avoid wasting space, as near right. First, sort the prints out into logical sequences. Then juggle them around on the page until you find an attractive layout, as far right. Mix print sizes and formats and consider how the colors and shapes in your shots relate to one another. If the album has dark pages, use self-adhesive labels for captioning.

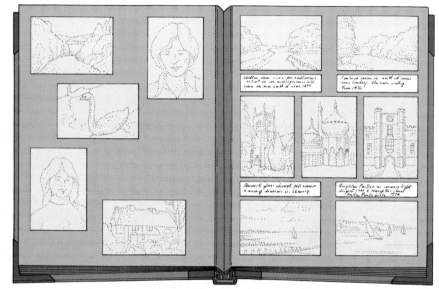

Mounting album prints
Some albums have ready-made methods for holding prints, such as self-adhesive pages with a cling-plastic overlay, **1**, or slit corners, **2**.

If your album has plain pages, you can, **3**, mount prints with double-sided adhesive or rubber cement. Or use opaque, **4**, or transparent, **5**, self-adhesive corners.

Dry mounting
Use the dry mounting method to mount larger prints. Attach a piece of shellac tissue to the center back of your print, using a cool iron. Trim off excess tissue and position the print carefully on the card mount. Hold it in place while you iron the tissue to the mount at all four corners. Then cover the print with a piece of thin card and iron the whole print, pressing firmly.

Displaying your prints

Use this list to help you choose from the vast array of print display methods on the market.

1 Traditional album — the best way of displaying a large collection of prints

2 Double-sided photo frame for twin portraits

3 Plastic frame in various different sizes

4 Decorative silver frame — costly and the best for romantic portrait or wedding shot

5 Wood-rimmed frame with glass — various sizes

6 Mini album with slip-in plastic sleeves — for carrying in pocket or bag

7 Your personal greeting card — made by mounting a favorite print on to a folded piece of card

8 Pocket album with slip-in plastic sleeves — prints inserted back to back

9 Plastic cube — displays five prints simultaneously

Showing slides

If you use slide film, it is worth buying a projector and screen to show them. Projecting slides brings out their brilliant colors and enlarges your shots almost to life size. There is a wide variety of projectors available, ranging from cheap, hand-operated models to more advanced types, like the projector right, that can change slides by remote control and focus automatically. If you can't afford a ready-made screen, improvise with a white, emulsion-painted wall or a large piece of mat, white card. When planning a show, edit your slides carefully, then arrange them in sequence in the projector tray. A hand viewer, right, is useful for previewing slides.

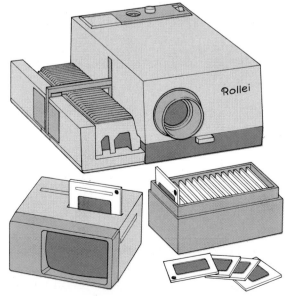

Slide storage/marking

Always store mounted slides in boxes or trays to protect them from damp and dust. Mark each mount in the bottom, left-hand corner, as shown left. Load your slides into the projector tray with the mark top right, facing the tray rear. Your slides will then be the right way around.

Filters/Accessories/Pocket SLRs

Filters change a subject's appearance by altering the nature, quality, or color of light reaching the film. Most are made of glass, mounted in a metal surround that screws into or clips on to the lens. Filters are available in various sizes, to fit most 126 and 35 mm camera lenses. 110 camera owners can tape filters over the lens, or improvise with a colored piece of gelatin held over the lens while shooting.

Cross-screen filter
This has a criss-cross grid that makes highlights look star-shaped. Use it for scenes with bright lights or reflections, as above.

UV filter
This filter absorbs ultra-violet light and cuts through haze, improving definition and color, especially of distant views. Like a skylight filter, it also helps to neutralize a blue cast. Compare the pictures above — the front shot, taken with the filter on, shows better definition and truer colors than the one behind. A UV filter left on a camera protects the lens.

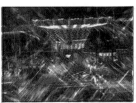

Using a colored filter
Single-color filters produce an overall color cast, as shown above. But unlike other filters featured here, they absorb so much light that you must compensate by increasing exposure. A number, called the "filter factor" indicates the exact adjustment required. If your camera has exposure symbols, select the next symbol down from the one indicated, e.g. "haze" instead of "sun". Exposure is adjusted automatically when the "eye" of a metering camera is on the lens and so covered by the filter. But when it is on the camera body, you must increase exposure by the recommended filter factor. Use these filters with slide film only — bulk-processors correct color casts on prints.

Skylight filter
This pale pink filter helps to counteract the blue color cast that occurs when the sky is clear blue or overcast. It also reduces UV light and haze. Use one particularly for seascapes and mountain scenery. Its effect is shown above. Shadows look very blue and definition is poor in the rear picture. Using a skylight filter has produced a crisper and warmer look.

Diffraction filter
This is a colorless filter that splits or "diffracts" rays of light into bursts of rainbow colors, as above.

Creating soft-focus
A "soft-focus" or slightly blurred picture is often more evocative than a pin-sharp image. To create soft-focus you must find a way of diffusing the light entering the camera. Ready-made diffusing filters soften shapes and colors evenly over the whole frame. But you can easily simulate their effect by improvising. Try shooting through a steamed-up window or breathing on a plain filter over the lens.

A thin layer of grease smeared on a UV filter gives a less even, soft-focus effect. In the shot above, it has blurred the lights and helped to convey the mood of twilight. Clean the filter after use with detergent and a cloth.

You can also soften an image by tying a piece of material over the lens. Any semi-transparent material, such as net or muslin, will do. A nylon stocking was used for the flower shot above, to mute colors and enhance the petals' soft texture.

Useful accessories

1 A soft shoulder bag, lined with foam is a cheap and convenient hold-all for equipment.

2 A hard-sided "gadget bag", with separate compartments for camera, flash and films, offers complete protection against knocks, dirt and rainy weather.

3 The Agfa Natarix close-up kit clips over the viewfinder and lens of some 110 cameras. It enables you to shoot as close as 19½ in (50 cm) and includes a gray filter to prevent overexposure in flash close-ups.

4 A metal or rubber lens hood reduces flare in bright sun and protects the lens from dust, rain and spray.

110 SLR cameras
The two cameras shown here are SLR or single lens reflex cameras. Unlike other pocket cameras, they allow you to see through the viewfinder exactly what the lens sees. This means that you can frame even your close-up subjects very precisely.

The Pentax Auto 110
The Auto 110, shown right, features a set of three interchangeable lenses. Besides a normal and a telephoto lens, it also has a "wide-angle" lens. This encompasses a broader view than normal and is useful for interiors and panoramas. Exposure is fully automatic — ranging from 1 sec at f2.8 to 1/750 at f13.5. Its accessories include an electronic flashgun, close-up lenses, filters and an autowinder. This winds on the film automatically, enabling you to take a sequence of shots without removing the camera from your eye.

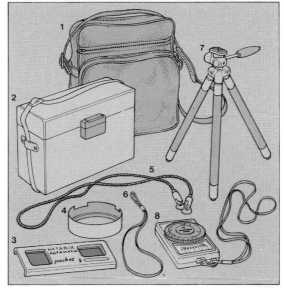

5 A strong neck strap leaves your hands free while carrying the camera. If you shorten the strap and tension it around your neck while shooting, it will help to reduce camera shake.

6 A wrist strap is useful for carrying a camera. Wrap it around your hand when you take pictures to help keep the camera steady.

7 A small, lightweight, collapsible tripod gives firm support against camera shake (p.17). It is especially useful for dusk or night shots which require slow shutter speeds.

8 A hand-held exposure meter enables you to take more selective readings from a scene than a built-in exposure meter.

Minolta 110 Zoom SLR
The main feature of this camera is its zoom lens — you can change from "normal" to "telephoto" simply by turning the lens focusing ring. A further twist of the ring brings a close-up lens into operation, which allows you to shoot as near as 12 in (30 cm) away. Exposure is semi-automatic — you set the aperture and the camera chooses the appropriate shutter speed — from 1/1000 sec to 10 full seconds for low light photography.

Index

Acknowledgments

**All photographs by
Andrew de Lory except:
Adrian Bailey** 4; 71tl **Clive
Boursnell** 40bl, br **David
Bradfield** 19 except box; 26–7;
32; 33 except box; 54–5; 60–1
Amy Carroll 15c **John Cleare**
80t, bl; 81tl, tr **Bruce Coleman**
82tl **Christopher Davis** 44br
L.R. Dawson/Bruce Coleman
83t **Christopher Dorling** 2
**Neville Fox-Davies/Bruce
Coleman** 82br **Frank Hermann**
41bl, br **Sarah King** 36 except
b; 37 except tr **Michael
Langford** 71tr, 2nd row l, 3rd
row c; 79bl, br **John Loughran**
44bl **Peter Loughran** 80br; 83
2nd row c, r, bc **David Moreby**
84bl, br; 85cl, cr **Michael
Newton** 29tl **David Pearson** 3;
47tl; 71tc, bc; 73r; 75cr, b **Erik
Pelham** 29cl; 42–3; 48–9; 52–3;
56 except bl; 57; 58–9; 64–5; 87
2nd row c **Roger Perry** 33 box t;
66 except bl **Roger Pring** 44t;
83bl **John Shaw/Bruce
Coleman** 83cl **Tim Stephens** 70
br **Peter Tucker** 46bl **Hazel
Wilkinson** 45 **J. Godfrey Wood**
11; 14t; 29cr; 34cl; 39r; 72cl, box;
74; 75tr, cl; 83br

**Dorling Kindersley and the
author** thank all the people who
have helped to produce this
book; including camera
manufacturers and distributors
(especially Agfa, Kodak and
Olympus), Charles Elliott, Paul
Hitchens and Roger Twigg,
Harry Pepper, John Marshall of
Smeets, Pelling and Cross Ltd.,
D.G. Leisure Centre
Illustrations by:
Norman Lacey M.I.S.T.C.
Diagrams by: Gary Marsh
Photographic services by:
Paulo Colour and Negs
Typesetting services by:
Filmtype Services Alphabet
Origination services by
City Engraving
Props and locations by:
London Contemporary Dance
Theatre, Mishkenot
Sha'ananim, Jerusalem,
Poynters Riding Stables,
Guards Polo Club, MG
Owners' Club